MW01177828

Homemade Dog Treat Recipes

Quick and Easy Treats to Make for Your Dog

© All Rights Reserved

Contents

Introduction

Thank you for buying this book, your dog will thank you for it.

I will be donating a portion of any profits made from sales of the book to a dog rescue charity each month.

Between us we will be helping some of the desperate dogs who are abused and dumped by people who have no heart. Every donation, however small, helps to rehabilitate, heal and rehome a dog who has nowhere to call home without the wonderful people who run these charities.

Our dogs are lucky, they have us to love them, feed them and make them delicious treats. Sales of this book will, in a small way, help those poor dogs who don't have anyone to care.

Anyone who loves dogs wants the very best they can afford for their best friend – I know I do. Have you ever looked on the back of a pack of commercially produced dog treats? Well, I bought a pack of 7 'twists' (dog treats) to see what they contain.

Here is the list of ingredients:

Derivatives of vegetable origin
Cereals
Meat and animal derivatives
Vegetable protein extracts
Various sugars
Minerals
Milk and milk derivatives (including 0.3% cheese)

The blurb on the front of the pack says, '*flavored with beef and cheese*', they don't mention (unless you read the ingredient list) the tiny amounts nor where the flavorings come from, just that they are derivatives, (*derivative ~ a substance or compound obtained from, or regarded as derived from, another substance or compound*).

So, although it says 'flavored with beef' it actually means that the beef is a flavoring *derived* from beef.

This pack wasn't the cheaper option either, it cost me £1.79 (around $2.88).

I know that I would rather give my best girl, Paula the whippet, the best food and treats that I can. If I'm going to give her a treat I want it to be something healthy and I want to know where the ingredients came from.

Paula

So I decided to make my own treats for her and got to work on doing some research for recipes she would like. This book is the result of my efforts.

I have left lots of white space for you to make notes or add your own recipes.

You can change the recipes around, as I did, by adding your own favorite ingredients or miss out the things that you know don't agree with your dog.

There is no yield given for any of the recipes because it really depends on how big you want your treats, Chihuahua size, Irish Wolfhound size or any size in between.

If you have a dog that is food sensitive, make a small batch of your chosen recipe by halving the ingredients and give your dog a little piece to see how he reacts. If he doesn't show an adverse reaction you can make a larger batch.

I love making dog treats and make lots at Christmas time, put them in a cellophane bag and tie with a pretty ribbon to give to my friends for their dogs.

After all, your dog is part of the family and should have a few gifts under the tree.

If you like this book you may also like my new Dog Treat Recipes – Book Two.

It is now available www.bit.ly/dtbk2 - UK
Or www.bit.ly/dtus - US

Grains

There are some dogs that don't tolerate grains, but that shouldn't stop you from making some special treats if your dog is one of those. You may need to use one of the grain free alternatives available. You can easily adapt these recipes by substituting a grain free flour for the regular flour.

Below are some you could use instead

Rice flour
Quinoa
Tapioca
Oat flour (make your own by blitzing oats in a food processor)
Amaranth
Potato flour
Millet flour

Sometimes these alternatives don't bind ingredients together as well as flours made with grain, so experiment with the ingredients. Use a beaten egg or some coconut oil to help to bind the ingredients together. You may also need to experiment a little with the amount of flour you use. So add the substitute flour slowly to get the right consistency for the recipe you are making.

You Know You're a Dog Lover When...

You think your dog is a good kisser,

Your dog has more clothes than you do,

You hang out with your dog instead of your friends,

You only go places your dog is welcome,

You eat fast food and your dog eats gourmet food,

You have more pictures of your dog than your family,

You spend more time on your dog's grooming than your own,

Your dog has more toys than your children,

You arrange your life around your dog's routine.

All for the love of your dog!

~ Author Unknown

Coconut Oil

There are a variety of oils you can use to benefit your dogs health, each with different benefits.

Coconut oil is my favorite and the one that I use regularly in the dog treats that I make.

Coconut oil consists of more than 90% saturated fats. Most of the saturated fats in coconut oil are Medium Chain Triglycerides (MCTs) which are good for you. Although there is currently no scientific proof, if fed regularly to your dog, it is said coconut oil may help:

...clear up skin conditions such as eczema, contact dermatitis and itchy skin

...reduce allergic reactions and improves skin health

...encourage sleek and shiny coats

...prevent and treat yeast and fungal infections

...disinfect cuts and promotes wound healing when applied topically

...the healing of cuts, wounds, hot spots, dry skin and hair, bites and stings when applied topically

...improve digestion and nutrient absorption

...healing of digestive disorders like inflammatory bowel syndrome and colitis

...reduce or eliminate bad breath in dogs

...prevent infection and disease because it contains powerful antibacterial, antiviral, and anti-fungal agents.

...regulate and balance insulin and promote normal thyroid function

...prevent or control diabetes

There are many ways you can give coconut oil to your dog; you can add it to their food, you can feed it from a spoon (lots of dogs love it, but not my girl...) or you can incorporate coconut oil in the homemade treats.

It is well worth adding coconut oil to your dog treats.

Just My Dog

"He is my other eyes that can see above the clouds; my other ears that hear above the winds.

He is the part of me that can reach out into the sea.

He has told me a thousand times over that I am his reason for being;

by the way he rests against my leg;

by the way he thumps his tail at my smallest smile;

by the way he shows his hurt when I leave without taking him. (I think it makes him sick with worry when he is not along to care for me.)

When I am wrong, he is delighted to forgive.

When I am angry, he clowns to make me smile.

When I am happy, he is joy unbounded.

When I am a fool, he ignores it.

When I succeed, he brags.

Without him, I am only another man.

With him, I am all-powerful.

He is loyalty itself.

He has taught me the meaning of devotion.

With him, I know a secret comfort and a private peace.

He has brought me understanding where before I was ignorant.

His head on my knee can heal my human hurts.

His presence by my side is protection against my fears of dark and unknown things.

He has promised to wait for me... whenever... wherever - in case I need him.

And I expect I will - as I always have.

He is just my dog."

~ *Gene Hill*

Turmeric for Your Dog

There has been a lot written about the benefits of adding turmeric to your own diet and it is thought to be an excellent addition to the diet of dogs and horses, in fact I am definitely a convert.

Briefly, (because this book is about dogs...) after 20+ years of burning pain in my shoulders (the left one particularly), the best the doctors could offer was painkillers and the only one that did any good was a codeine based one.

I heard about a Facebook group that talks about the health benefits of turmeric and joined. Not being a curry fan I didn't fancy making a turmeric drink so I bought a capsule maker, black pepper and some turmeric powder (minimum 3% curcumin content) and made capsules. After around 6 weeks I suddenly realised that I had not taken any painkillers for a month...

The Facebook group also has a lot of success stories about the use of turmeric for various problems in dogs and horses.

Just type '**Turmeric User Group**' into the search bar on Facebook.

You will find lots of information on the benefits of giving turmeric to your dog and the recipe for a super paste to add to his food.

The Special Training Treat Tray

When training a new puppy or an older dog it is good to have some 'high value' treats for just those occasions.

High value treats would be something that your dog loves, for my girl it is sausages, cheese and chicken. Of course, this will only work if your dog is food orientated.

Buy a bag of the very cheap frozen sausages from the supermarket and cook them all on a tray when cooking a family dinner. Leave to cool and cut into very small pieces.

Lay them flat on a tray and freeze.

When frozen put them into small bags and leave in the freezer until you need them.

Take a bag out of the freezer an hour or so before you are going to use them.

Liver is another cheap meat that most dogs love. Any bits of cheese that are past their best or cheese rinds get chopped up into small cubes and added to the tray in the freezer. Also any leftover meat from dinner could be cut into small pieces and added to the tray.

Whatever it is that your dog would do anything for can be chopped up and added to the freezer tray.

Only use the 'special treats' for training and your dog will soon be doing whatever you ask...

Sweet Potato Rounds

Ingredients

2 medium size sweet potatoes
½ cup your choice of flour
¼ cup gelatin powder
1 cup coconut oil
Water as needed to get the right consistency

Method

Preheat the oven to 350°.

Cook and mash the sweet potatoes. Leave to cool.

Put all ingredients into a bowl and mix until well incorporated. If needed, add a little extra flour to get a dough that comes together.

Wet your hands to avoid the dough sticking and roll into balls and flatten with your hand. You decide how big you want your treats. Put onto a lightly greased baking tray.

Bake for 20 minutes until slightly browned round the edges.

Remove from oven and let cool completely before removing from the baking tray.

You can store these in an air-tight container in the fridge for several weeks or freeze for several months.

__Having a dog will bless you with the happiest days of your life, and one of the worst days.__ ~ *Author Unknown*

Baked Meaty Biscuits

Ingredients

1kg ground chicken or beef
1 egg, beaten
½ cup oatmeal or cooked brown rice
Grated carrot
1 teaspoon fresh ground black pepper
1 tablespoon cider vinegar

Method

Combine all ingredients until well mixed by pulsing in a blender.

Wet your hands to stop the mixture sticking to them and roll into small balls.

Place on a baking tray and flatten lightly.

Bake until crisp.

This recipe will make a lot of small biscuit treats so freeze them in bags until you need them.

You can substitute the carrot for any vegetable your dog likes such as broccoli, cabbage, green beans, spinach etc. But no onion, it is toxic to dogs.

"If you think dogs can't count, try putting three dog biscuits in your pocket and then giving him only two of them." ~ *Phil Pastoret*

Banana Sweet Breath Biscuits

Ingredients

1 banana, mashed
½ cup peanut butter
¼ cup wheat-germ or rice flour
½ cup chopped parsley
½ tablespoon coconut oil
Warm water

Method

Preheat oven to 180° or 325°. Mix together the banana, peanut butter, chopped parsley, coconut oil and flour.

Add as much warm water as you need to make a firm dough.

Roll out on a floured board about 1 inch thick.

Use cookie cutters to make biscuit shapes

Place on non-stick tray and bake in the oven for 10 to 15 minutes.

Take them out and let them cool on a wire rack.

Cheesy Dog Cubes

Ingredients

1½ cups whole wheat flour (or rice flour)
1¼ cups grated cheddar cheese
¼ pound margarine
Water

Method

Put the grated cheese into a bowl and let stand until it reaches room temperature.

Cream the cheese with the softened margarine and flour. Add enough water to form the mixture into a ball.

Chill in the refrigerator for at least an hour. Roll out on a floured board. Cut into cubes and bake at 375° for around 15-20 minutes or until slightly brown and firm.

Turn the oven off and leave the treats to cool in the oven. You will find that these treats will firm up as they cool.

"Whoever said you can't buy happiness forgot little puppies." ~ *Gene Hill*

Carrot Treats

Ingredients

2 cups whole wheat flour
½ cup quinoa
¼ teaspoon garlic powder
1 cup grated carrot
1 cup cooked brown rice
3 tablespoons coconut oil
½ cup water

Method

Combine flour, quinoa, garlic powder and grated carrot. Add cooked rice and coconut oil. Combine well. Add the water slowly and mix well until the dough is easy to handle, not crumbly. Add more coconut oil or water if needed to achieve the proper consistency.

Lightly flour the board and roll out dough to ¼ inch thickness. Cut with a cookie cutter.

Bake at 350° for 25 minutes.

Leave to cool on wire rack.

"Once you have had a wonderful dog, a life without one, is a life diminished."

~ *Dean Koontz*

Beef Biscuits

Ingredients

2½ cups whole wheat flour
½ teaspoon garlic powder
6 tablespoons beef fat
1 egg
½ cup cold water

Method

Preheat oven to 350°. Lightly oil a cookie sheet.

Combine flour and garlic powder. Stir in meat fat until mixture resembles corn meal.

Lightly beat the egg and add to the mixture. Add enough water so that mixture forms a ball.

Using your fingers, pat out dough onto cookie sheet to about ½ inch thick. Cut with cookie cutter or knife and remove trimmed bits. Roll the trimmings into a ball and do the same again until all the mixture is used.

Bake for around 25 – 30 minutes. Remove from tray and cool on rack.

NOTES

Apple Crisp

Ingredients

2 cups whole wheat flour
1 cup cornmeal
1 apple grated
1 egg beaten
1/3 cup coconut oil
1 tablespoon honey
1 tablespoon cider vinegar
½ cup warm water

Method

Add the honey to the warm water and stir to dissolve, leave to cool.

Preheat oven to 350°. Lightly grease a cookie sheet.

Lightly dust work surface with flour.

Blend flour and cornmeal in a large mixing bowl.

Add apple, egg, oil, cider vinegar, honey and water and mix until the ingredients are combined.

On floured surface, roll dough out to about ½ inch thick. Cut with cookie cutters of desired shape and size. Place the treats on the prepared sheet.

Bake in preheated oven 25 – 30 minutes. Turn off oven.

Leave door closed for around 1 hour to allow the treats to crisp up.

Store baked treats in airtight container or plastic bag and place in refrigerator or freezer.

Apple Cinnamon Dog Biscuits

Ingredients

1 pack dried apple
1 teaspoon cinnamon – Ceylon cinnamon is best.
1 tablespoon parsley, freeze-dried or fresh
1 tablespoon garlic powder
1 cup ice water
½ cup Corn Oil
5 cups flour
½ cup powdered milk
2 eggs
1 tablespoon coconut oil

Method

Blitz the apples in a food processor so the pieces are small.

Combine all the ingredients in a large bowl. You can add more coconut oil or water if dough is too dry.

Using a floured rolling pin, roll out dough to about ½ inch thick (you can make them thinner or thicker).

Using a cookie cutter, cut into shapes and place on lightly greased cookie sheets. Bake at 350°

for approximately 20 – 25 minutes or until
golden brown.

Leave on a wire rack to cool.

Sardine Special

Ingredients

2½ cups whole wheat flour
½ cup non-fat milk powder
1 teaspoon garlic powder
1 egg
1 tin sardines in oil

Method

Combine flour, powdered milk and garlic powder in a medium sized bowl. Add beaten egg and mix well. Break up the sardines into small pieces then add to the mixture along with the oil from the sardines and mix until well incorporated. Dough should be stiff enough to roll out. If necessary add a little coconut oil or water.

On a well-floured surface, roll out dough to around ¼ inch thickness. Cut with shaped cookie cutter.

Place biscuits on cookie sheets and bake at 350° for 30 minutes.

Leave to cool on wire rack.

"Dogs feel very strongly that they should always go with you in the car, in case the need should arise for them to bark violently at nothing right in your ear."

~ Dave Barry

Baby Food Canine Cookies

Ingredients

3 jars baby food – beef, chicken or vegetable variety
¼ cup flour of your choice
¼ cup dry milk powder

Method

Combine ingredients in bowl and mix well.

With wet hands, roll into small balls and place on well-greased cookie sheet.

Flatten slightly.

Bake for around 15 minutes or until brown.

Cool on a wire rack and store in the refrigerator. Freezes well.

Barking Bacon Bits

Ingredients

3 cups whole wheat flour
½ cup milk
1 egg
¼ cup coconut oil
4 slices bacon
½ cup cold water

Method

Preheat oven to 350°

Cook bacon until crisp. Leave to go cold then crumble into small pieces.

Beat the egg and add the milk, coconut oil and water and mix well.

Add the crumbled bacon and flour and mix ingredients together thoroughly.

Roll out on a floured surface to ½ - ¼ inch thickness. Cut into small bite sized pieces or you could use a cookie cutter.

Bake on a lightly greased baking sheet for 35 – 40 minutes or until cooked and golden.

Turn oven off and leave to cool in oven to crisp
up.

Bacon and Egg Treats

Ingredients

6 slices crisp cooked bacon crumbled
4 eggs, well beaten
1/8 cup bacon grease or coconut oil
1 cup water
½ cup powdered milk
2 cups whole wheat flour
2 cups wheat germ
½ cup cornmeal

Method

Preheat the oven to 350°.

Mix all ingredients together in a blender, pulsing until everything is well distributed.

The mixture will be a dropping consistency.

Put heaped teaspoonfuls of the mixture onto a lightly greased baking sheet.

Bake for around 15 minutes.

Turn the oven off and leave cookies on baking sheet in the oven overnight to dry out.

Note: This recipes makes a lot of treats so you could halve the ingredients if you want to make a smaller batch.

Liver Lovelies

Ingredients

1¼ lbs liver
2 cups wheat germ
2 tablespoons whole wheat flour
1 cup cooked barley
2 eggs
3 tablespoons peanut butter
1 clove garlic
1 tablespoon coconut oil

Method

Pre heat oven to 350°.

Blend liver and garlic clove until it is a smooth paste. Add the eggs and peanut butter and blend again until smooth.

In separate bowl mix together the wheat germ, whole wheat flour, and cooked barley. Add the blended liver mixture and coconut oil and mix until ingredients are well combined.

Pour the mixture into a greased 9 x 9 baking dish and bake for around 20 minutes or until cooked.

When cool cut into treat sized pieces.

Store in refrigerator or freezer.

Beefy Twisters

Ingredients

3½ cups your choice of flour
1 cup cornmeal
1 pack unflavored gelatin
¼ cup milk
1 egg
¼ cup coconut oil
1 jar meat based baby food
¾ cup warm beef stock

Method

Preheat oven to 400°.

Sift dry ingredients into large bowl.

Add milk, egg, oil, baby food and beef stock.
Stir until well mixed.

When the dough is workable, roll out on a
lightly floured surface to ¼ inch thick.

Cut in ¼ inch by 3 inch strips, twisting each
strip 3 turns before placing on cookie sheet.

Bake for around 35 – 40 minutes. Store in
refrigerator

Cheese & Vegetable Chewies

Ingredients

½ cup grated cheese
3 tablespoons vegetable oil or coconut oil
3 teaspoons applesauce
½ cup vegetables of your choice
1 clove garlic
1 cup flour of your choice – I prefer wholewheat for this recipe
Water as needed

Method

Preheat oven to 350°.

Mix cheese, oil and applesauce together.

Chop or crush the garlic.

Add the vegetables, garlic, and flour to the cheese mixture. Combine thoroughly.

Add just enough water to help form a ball. Cover and chill for one hour.

Sprinkle some flour on a board. Roll out to around ½ inch thick and cut into shapes.

Bake for around 15 minutes or until golden brown.

Cool on a wire rack.

Anybody who doesn't know what soap tastes like never washed a dog.

~ Franklin P. Jones

10 Dog Wishes

1. My life is likely to last 10 to 15 years. Any separation from you will be very painful. My wish is that you don't desert me.

2. Give me time to understand what you want of me. Place your trust in me - it is crucial for my well-being.
   My wish is to please you.

3. Don't be angry with me for long and don't lock me up as punishment. You have your work, your friends, your entertainment. I have only you.
   My wish is to be important to you.

4. Talk to me. Even if I don't understand your words, I understand your voice when it's speaking to me.
   My wish is to understand everything you say to me.

5. Be aware that however you treat me, I'll never forget it.
   My wish is that you treat me as you would like to be treated.

6. Before you hit me, remember that I have teeth that could easily crush the bones in your hand, but I choose not to bite you.

My wish is that you are as kind to me as I am to you.

7. Before you scold me for being lazy or uncooperative, ask yourself if something might be bothering me. Perhaps I'm not getting the right food, I've been out in the sun too long, or my heart may be getting old and weak.
My wish is that you try and understand my needs.

8. Take care of me when I get old. You, too, will grow old.
My wish is to grow old with you.

9. Go with me on my final difficult journey. Never say, "I can't bear to watch it" or "Let it happen in my absence." Please hold me while I go over to the Rainbow Bridge. Everything is easier for me if you are there.
My wish is that you will care enough to help me when I am too tired or ill to carry on.

10. Remember, I love you.
My wish is that you love me too.

Adapted from a poem © Stan Rawlinson 1993

Barkley's Birthday Cake

Ingredients

1½ cups all-purpose
flour
1½ teaspoons baking
powder
½ cup soft butter
½ cup corn oil
1 jar meat based
baby food
4 eggs
2 or 3 strips beef
jerky

Method

Preheat oven to 325°.

Grease and line an 8 x 5 x 3 inch loaf pan.

Cream butter until smooth, add corn oil, baby
food, and eggs. Beat until smooth.

Add dry ingredients to the butter mixture and
mix well until batter is smooth.

Crumble beef jerky and fold into batter.

Pour batter into loaf pan. Bake for around 1 hour and 10 minutes.

Cool on wire rack in loaf pan before removing. Allow to go completely cold before icing with plain yogurt or cottage cheese. You could decorate with strips of cooked bacon.

In the unlikely event of there being any leftovers, store uneaten cake in refrigerator.

Bread Machine Biscuits

Ingredients

¾ cup stock – beef, chicken or vegetable
1 egg
3 tablespoons coconut oil
1 cup all-purpose flour
1 cup whole wheat flour
1/3 cup quinoa
1/3 cup bran
¼ cup nonfat dry milk
¼ teaspoon garlic powder
1½ teaspoons yeast

Method

This is a great recipe of you have a bread machine.

Add ingredients to the bread pan and use the "Dough" cycle.

When machine beeps, remove dough to lightly floured board and roll out to around ¼ inch thick.

Using a cookie cutter, cut out the biscuits and place on a lightly greased cookie sheet. Re-roll scraps and repeat till all dough is used up. Place in a warm location and let rise 30 minutes.

Bake at 325° for around 30 minutes until brown and crisp. Place on a rack to cool. Store in an airtight container.

The Best Part about Owning a Dog...

... is the way he will come over to see you, for no reason, just to let you know you're important to him

... is the way he is always ready to lick the jelly off your nose...

... is the way he looks into your eyes and finds contentment in simply being near you

... is the way he will run all over the yard, fetch a soggy tennis ball and bring it back to you as if to say "look mom, it's all have, but it's yours

... is the way he wakes you up in the morning by pushing his cold wet nose in your ear and snuffing loudly

... is the way he shreds toilet paper all over the house, because it's fun even though he knows he shouldn't

... is the way he's sure he can catch the ducks in the lake today...

... is the way he comes over to you when he is sad

... is the way he wedges himself near you when you are sad and pushes all others away, to console you with his love

... is the way he pounces on crickets in the backyard

... is the way he looks perplexed when the crickets escape

... is the way he is terrified of the evil pink hula hoop

... is the way he doesn't care about your bad hair days

... is the way he loves you, even when you are impatient with him and have no time this morning for a game of tug-a-war

... is the way his coat feels like liquid silk under your fingers

... is the way he finds wisdom beyond words

... is the way your life has been transformed since he came bounding into your life

~ Author Unknown

Cookie Cakes

Ingredients

2 cups whole wheat flour
½ cup flour
1 cup skimmed milk or water
1 tablespoon honey
1 tablespoon oil
1 teaspoon sea salt – optional

Method

Mix dry ingredients.

Add liquid and honey.

Mix and let the dough rest in a warm place for 15 minutes. Add oil and allow to sit another 1/2 hour.

Take walnut size portions of dough and flatten into small cakes.

Bake in oven at 400° for around 30 minutes.

"If you can look at a puppy and not feel instant love and affection – you must be a cat..." ~ Author Unknown

Best Biscuits

Ingredients

2½ cups whole wheat flour
1 teaspoon brown sugar
½ cup powdered milk
6 tablespoons butter
½ teaspoon salt
1 egg
½ teaspoon garlic powder
½ cup cold water

Method

Combine the flour, milk, salt, garlic powder and sugar. Cut in butter until mixture resembles cornmeal, you could pulse in a food processor.

Beat the egg and mix in, then add enough cold water to make a ball.

Pat dough to ½ inch thick on a lightly oiled cookie sheet. Cut out shapes with a cookie cutter or biscuit cutter and bake on cookie sheet for 25 minutes at around 350°. Remove from the oven and cool on a wire rack.

When you add the egg you could add grated vegetables, ground meat or whatever takes you fancy. Use your imagination.

A Dog's Prayer

Treat me kindly, my beloved master, for no heart in all the world is more grateful for kindness than the loving heart of me.

Do not break my spirit with a stick, for though I should lick your hand between the blows, your patience and understanding will more quickly teach me the things you would have me do.

Speak to me often, for your voice is the world's sweetest music, as you must know by the fierce wagging of my tail when your footstep falls upon my waiting ear.

When it is cold and wet, please take me inside for I am now a domesticated animal, no longer used to bitter elements. I ask no greater glory than the privilege of sitting at your feet beside the hearth, though had you no home, I would rather follow you through ice and snow than rest upon the softest pillow in the warmest home in all the land for you are my god and I am your devoted worshiper.

Keep my dish filled with fresh water, for although I should not reproach you were it dry, I cannot tell you when I suffer thirst.

Feed me clean food, that I may stay well, to romp and play and do your bidding, to walk by your side, and stand ready, willing and able to protect you with my life, should your life be in danger.

And, beloved master, should the Great Master see fit to deprive me of my health or sight, do not turn me away from you.

Rather hold me gently in your arms as skilled hands grant me the merciful boon of eternal rest and I will leave you knowing with the last breath I drew, my fate was ever safest in your hands.

~ Beth Norman Harris

Chicken Cookies

Ingredients

2 cups whole wheat flour
2/3 cup yellow cornmeal
2 tablespoons coconut oil
½ cup chicken broth
2 eggs
¼ cup low-fat milk
1 egg

Method

Heat oven to 350°.

In a large bowl, mix together flour and cornmeal. Beat the eggs and mix in the chicken broth and oil.

Add the wet ingredients to the dry ingredients and mix well. The dough should be firm.

Place in refrigerator for around 15 minutes.

On a lightly floured surface, roll out dough to around ¼ inch thick.

Using cookie cutters cut into shapes and brush with beaten egg. Place on lightly greased baking tray.

Bake for 25-35 minutes, until golden brown.

Remove and leave to cool on the baking tray.
Store in airtight container.

Canine Popsicles

Ingredients

32 ounces vanilla yogurt
1 cup peanut butter
Handful of kibble
Paper cupcake cases

Method

Put the peanut butter in a microwave safe dish and microwave until melted stirring at regular intervals. Allow to cool slightly.

Mix the yogurt, kibble and melted peanut butter together until well combined.

Pour the mixture into cupcake papers and freeze. It is best to put the paper cases in a cupcake tin so they won't collapse or you could put the mixture directly into the cupcake tin without the paper cases. You will have to put the tin in hot water to release the popsicles then put them back in the freezer until you want to use them.

These are a great treat for when the weather is really hot. Instead of kibble you could add small pieces of cooked chicken, small squares of cheese, chopped sausages – in fact you can add anything your dog enjoys.

The Story of Creation

On the first day, God created the dog.

On the second day, God created man to serve
the dog.

On the third day, God created all the animals of
the
earth to serve as potential food for the dog.

On the fourth day, God created honest toil so
that man
could labour for the good of the dog.

On the fifth day, God created the tennis ball so
that the
dog might or might not retrieve it.

On the sixth day, God created veterinary science
to
keep the dog happy and the man broke.

On the seventh day, God tried to rest, but he had
to
walk the dog.

Home Made Dog Cookies

Ingredients

1 pack active dry yeast
1 cup warm chicken broth
2 tablespoons coconut oil
1¾ cups all purpose flour
1½ cups whole wheat flour
1½ cups cracked wheat
½ cup cornmeal
½ cup milk powder
2 teaspoons garlic powder
1 tablespoon milk
1 egg – beaten

Method

Preheat oven to 300°.

Dissolve yeast in ¼ cup warm water as the pack instructions.

Stir in broth and coconut oil. Add 1 cup of all purpose flour, all the whole wheat flour, cracked wheat, cornmeal, dry milk, garlic powder and mix well.

On a floured board, knead in remaining flour. Leave to rest for 30 minutes.

Knead dough well. Roll out to around ¾ inch thick and cut into desired shapes.

Place on ungreased baking sheet, brush tops with beaten egg and milk mixture.

Bake for around 45 minutes or until golden brown.

Turn oven off and let dry overnight.

Garlic Cheese Bits

Ingredients

1 cup flour
1 cup cheddar cheese
1 tablespoon garlic powder
1 tablespoon butter
½ cup milk

Method

Preheat oven to 350°.
Grate the cheese and mix into the flour, add garlic powder and softened butter.

Slowly add milk till to form a stiff dough. When you get the required consistency stop adding the milk.

Knead on floured board for a few minutes.

Roll into small balls and place on ungreased cookie sheet. Lightly press down the balls and bake for around 15 minutes.

Leave to cool in the oven with the door slightly open until cold and firm.

Store in the refrigerator

Cheese and Carrot Cakes

Ingredients

2 cups flour
1 tablespoon baking powder
1 cup grated cheddar cheese
1 cup grated carrot
2 eggs
1 cup milk

Method

Preheat oven to 350°.

Grease a muffin tin or line it with paper baking cups. If you want to make smaller cakes you could use a tin with smaller compartments like those usually used for making candies. You can buy one on Amazon

Combine the flour and baking powder. Add the

cheese and carrots and use your fingers to mix
them into the flour until they are well-
distributed.

Beat the eggs, milk and vegetable oil together
well. Pour mixture over the flour mixture and
stir until just combined.

Fill the muffin cups three-quarters full with the
mixture. Bake for 15 – 20 minutes or until the
muffins feel springy.

No Wheat Treats

Ingredients

1 cup white rice flour
¼ cup soy flour
¼ cup egg substitute
1 tablespoon molasses
1/3 cup milk approximately
1/3 cup powdered milk
2 tablespoons coconut oil

Method

Preheat oven to 350°.

Mix the dry ingredients together then add the molasses, oil, egg and a little of the milk.

Mix until all the ingredients are well combined adding more milk as required to make a firm dough.

Roll out and cut into whatever shape you like and place on a lightly greased baking sheet.

Bake for around 20 minutes. Turn off oven and leave to cool. Store in tightly sealed container.

Liver and Bacon Treats

Ingredients

1 cup whole wheat flour
1 cup cornmeal
1/2 cup wheat germ
1 teaspoon garlic powder
1 pound beef liver
4 slices bacon

Method

Pre-heat oven to 350°. Grease a cookie sheet.

Chop bacon into very small pieces; use scissors, it's easier.

Liquefy liver in blender, add bacon and dry ingredients. Pulse until well combined.

Drop teaspoonfuls of mixture onto cookie sheet and flatten with a spoon dipped in water. Bake for 15-20 minutes.

Freezes well.

Thank you

This book is my small way of helping those dogs who need someone to care for them.

We all know there are countless dogs who are abused, unloved and homeless and need one of the charities to help find them a forever home.

By buying this book you have helped at least one of the charities who need lots of money to help these poor dogs find a better life – thank you.

If you know of anyone who is thinking of getting a dog, please try and convince them to adopt rather than buy.

If you are thinking of adding another dog to your own family, please do consider adoption.

But if you are wanting a pedigree puppy and can't find one at your local shelter, do your research and find a respected breeder who will show you the puppies with their Mom.

Be very wary of anyone who has excuses for not introducing you to the puppy's family. Be careful you are not fueling the ever increasing and reprehensible industry of puppy farming. NEVER buy a puppy that has to be shipped to you and have not seen, however cheap it seems. You could be buying into a whole heap of trouble.

But most importantly, love your dog.

**"You can say any foolish thing to a dog,
and the dog will give you a look that
says, 'Wow, you're right! I never
would've thought of that!'"**
~ *Dave Barry*

If Not For You...

(to the Rescuers from the Dogs you Saved)

I would've died that day if not for you.
I would've given up on life if not for your
kind eyes.
I would've used my teeth in fear if not for
your gentle hands.
I would have died believing that not one
human cares

I would have died believing there is no such
thing as fur that isn't matted,
skin that isn't flea bitten,
no such thing as enough food that I didn't
have to fight for,
I would have died not knowing there are soft
beds to sleep on,
Not knowing that someone could love me, to
show me I deserve to be loved just because I
exist.
Your kind eyes, your loving smile, your
gentle hands
Your big heart saved me...

You saved me from the terror of the pound,
Soothed away the memories of my old life.
You have taught me what it means to be
loved.

I have seen you do the same for other dogs
like me.
I have heard you ask yourself in times of
despair
Why you do it
When there is no more money, no more
room, no more homes
You open your heart a little bigger, stretch
the money a little tighter
Make just a little more room, to save one
more like me.
I tell you with the gratitude and love that
shines in my eyes
In the best way I know how
Reminding you why you go on trying.

I am the reason
The dogs before me are the reason
As are the ones who come after.
Our lives would've been wasted, our love
never given

We would have died if not for you...

~ *Author Unknown*

Dogs have a
way of finding
the people who
need them,
filling an
emptiness we
don't even
know we have

~ Thorn Jones

NOTES

DISCLAIMER

All information in the book is for general information purposes only.

The author has used her best efforts in preparing this information and makes no representations or warranties with respect to the accuracy, applicability or completeness of the material contained within.

The author shall in no event be held liable for losses or damages whatsoever. The author assumes no responsibility or liability for any consequences resulting directly or indirectly from any action or lack of action that you take based on the information in this document. Use of the publication and recipes therein is at your own risk.

Reproduction or translation of any part of this publication by any means, electronic or mechanical, without the permission of the author, is both forbidden and illegal. You are not permitted to share, sell, and trade or give away this document, it is for your own personal use only, unless stated otherwise.

The reader assumes full risk and responsibility for all actions taken as a result of the information contained within this book and the author will not be held responsible for any loss or damage, whether consequential, incidental, or otherwise that may result from the information presented in this book.

The author has relied on her own experiences when compiling this book and each recipe is tried and tested in her own kitchen.

By using any of the recipes in this publication, you agree that you have read the disclaimer and agree with all the terms.

Manufactured by Amazon.ca
Bolton, ON

17539584R00048